THE KISS

by
Robert Lebeck

ST. MARTIN'S PRESS
New York

For information, write: St. Martin's Press,
175 Fifth Avenue, New York, N.Y. 10010
Printed and bound in Italy by Officine Grafiche of Arnoldo Mondadori
Editore, Verona

Library of Congress Catalog Card Number: 80-51379
ISBN: 0-312-45687-5

Picture postcards first appeared at about the same time in France and Germany in the late nineteenth century, and by 1900 had become a huge worldwide enthusiasm. Almost immediately certain types of cards became collectors' items, and today picture postcards make up one of the most popular of collectibles. But one need not be a collector like Robert Lebeck (from whose vast archives the contents of this book were selected) to be charmed by the universal motif that characterizes THE KISS. Whether reproduced from the art of Rodin or Correggio or reflecting the sensibilities and romanticism of a historical period notable for sentimentality, these depictions of love and affection retain their appeal—but not always for the same reasons. Some of the cards included here seem more ridiculous than romantic: e.g., the hotheaded gentleman locked in an embrace on a card labled "Charity" (no. 10), and the rotund couple in *lederhosen* and peasant blouse (no. 80)—but perhaps they were always intended to! Some are comical ("Try it, it's good"—no. 43), cute (two kids in bathing suits—no. 22), or bizarre (the Atlantic kissing the Pacific through the Panama Canal—no. 23).

Yet other examples here take a more serious view of kissing. The chilling "Death and the Maiden" (no. 28) is all the more shocking for the tenderness with which Death embraces its young victim. "Passion" (no. 61) displays no cuteness, and the gentlemen in no. 64 is approaching decadence in his demenor and his hand movement, though the lady doesn't seem to mind.

It would be easy to sink into a morass of symbolic interpretations of the significance of the diversity of kissing illustrated here: anthropoligical, religious, philosophical and artistic. But it is clear to anyone with a reasonable perspective that these postcards were, for the most part, intended simply as expressions of romance or warm feelings, designed to be sent from one friend to another. Perhaps some pictorial messages were more laden with emotion than others, but in general the mood of these illustrations is either good humor or affection, and often both, and no greater reason need be given for their popularity today than this. It is indeed a tribute to the immortality of romantic love that these pictures continue to give pleasure—for whatever reason—almost a century after their creation.

The Publisher

1. Drawing by R. Rössler
No. 412—M.M. Vienne. M. Munk

 2219/20

2, 3, 4. Photographs. Series 2219/20, no further details

2219/20

2, 3, 4. Photographs. Series 2219/20, no further details

2219/20

5. Color lithograph, relief print
   5 Heller stamp, Vienna 27.4.1905

Milá Mařenko

Stanuli jsme v
blahém objetí,
Líbali se láskou vřelou.
Kdo začal dříve? Kdož to ví,
Přišlo to tak samo sebou.

přijmi ode mne srdečný
pozdrav a přejdi mé přání he mě ráda tě uvidím
s bohem R. F.

6. Color lithograph by P. Hegedüs-Geiger. About 1900

HEGEDÜS-
GEIGER-P.

7. Color lithograph, c. 1900

8. Color litho., relief print. S.I.B. series 240. About 1900

Gefangen, gefangen, Du Uebermut,
Jetzt bist Du mein siegreich erobertes Gut,
Nun gieb den Tribut: einen Kuss in Ähr'n,
Das weisst Du, Du Süsse, kann niemand wehr'n!

9. Color litho., relief print. Series 3915
   Postmark: Mitcheldean, England. 25.2.1905

10. *La Charite*. Color litho. Relief print. EAS
    Belgian lc. stamp. 18.11.1909. To Mynheer M. Vervoort in
    Hoboken

11. Color Litho.
   From Magdeburg 12.6.1902 to Frl. Nanny Landmann in
   Diesdorf

Gedenkst du Liebchen,
    der Stund
Die Küsse wir tauschten
        beglück
Wo wir von Mund zu
        Mund
Nur Worte der Liebe
        gesche...

12. *The Kiss.* Photograph. KHKG 1701/2

Der Kuss

13. Photograph. NVSB No. 1
    Dresden 1.10.1910

14. *Le Baiser*. Photograph. DIX 150

LE BAISER

DIX
150

15. Photograph. Noyer 2312

16. Sculpture by J.-B. Champeil. Photograph. 4787

4787. Парижъ. Салонъ — Весна любви. — Ж. Шамнеи.

17. *Electric Spark*. Sculpture by Reinhold Begas, Berlin
    Photograph. AE 2511

ELEKTRISCHER FUNKE.
ÉTINCELLE ÉLECTRIQUE.

Prof
REINHOLD BEGAS.
BERLIN.

Æ
2511.

18. *The Kiss.* Sculpture by Auguste Rodin (1840-1917). Photograph. Neue Photographische Gesellschaft, Berlin-Steglitz. 5246

Paris (Luxembourg). Le baiser par Rodin.

5246

19. *The Kiss.* Sculpture by Emil Renker. Photograph. Produced by Friedrich O. Wolter, Berlin W. 35.243

Emil Renker: DER KUSS.

20. *The First Kiss.* Sculpture by Andreoni. F.M.K. 2760
    Hamburg 23.7.1908 to Fräulein Gertrud Wedekind, Ottensen,
    Flottbeckerchaussee.

Der erste Kuss

F.M.K.
2760

ANDREONI

21. *Soldier's love is true love.* Photograph. WS SB. Series 695,
    picture 4
    Nordhausen 13.4.1917 to Fräulein Hedwig Sachs,
    Braunschweig, Südstr. 6/7 III

Treu ist die Soldatenliebe

22. Photograph. NPG (Neue Photographische Gesellschaft, Berlin-Steglitz) 2680
    Naval post
    Rüstringen (Oldenburg) 19.7.1916 to Fräulein Mariechen Kluckhuhn care of Frau Rechnungsrat Müller, Lemgo, Bismarckstrasse

2680

23. *The Kiss of the Oceans.* The meeting of the Atlantic and Pacific
    Technical details about the Panama Canal.
    Relief print.
    I.L. Maduro, Jr., Panama, No. 5881

Meeting of the
Atlantic and Pacific
"The Kiss of the
Oceans"

Canal Statistics.

Length . . . . 40 miles
Channel . . { width at top . . . 500 to 1000 ft.
            { " . . bottom . 300 to 650 ft.
Time of passage { Through Canal . . 10 hours
                { " . . . Locks . . 3 hours
            { Length of crest . . . . 8000 ft.
Gatun Dam { Extreme width . . . . 2600 ft.
          { Height above normal lake level 30 ft.
        { At Gatun . . . . 3 double sets | Average lift 32 ft.
Locks { " Pedro Miguel 1 double set | Length . . 1000 ft.
        { " Miraflores . . 2 double sets | Width . . 110 ft.
Culebra Cut . . . Length . . . . 9 miles
Total number of men employed 40,000
Estimated total cost . . . . $ 375,000,000
Area of Canal Zone . . . . 448 Sq. Miles

24. Reproduction of a painting by Wertheimer, *The Wave's Kiss*.
J. Plichta Salon, Prague, 1026

25. Reproduction of a painting by Antoine Joseph Wiertz
    (1806-1865): *The Intoxication of Love*. Wiertz Museum, Brussels.
    Color litho.
    Produced by Stengel, Dresden

26. *Triumph of Love*. "Cromoscultura" by Mastroianni.
   A. Traldi, Milan, No. 01828

27. Reproduction of a painting by Antonio Allegri (known as
    Correggio): *Jove embracing Io*. Vienna. Color litho.
    Produced by Stengel, Dresden, 29767

28. Reproduction of a painting by Adolf Hering: *Death and the Maiden*. Modern Masters series (publishers Arthur Rehn & Co., Berlin).
   To Fräulein Frieda Mulack, Berlin: "But we don't want to die! Your decrepit young man sends a sweet kiss!"

29. *Bacio sublime* "Cromoscultura" by Mastroianni. A. Traldi,
    Milan. No. 01301.
    Hungarian 8 filler stamp

30. *Romeo and Juliet*. Color litho.
    1907 from Verona to Barcelona

Romeo und Julie.

31. *Cheers, New Year*. Colored half-tone engraving. Series 319, picture 2. Vienna 31.12.1913.

 To Fräulein Marie Wanke, Landesversicherung, Löwelstrasse 19, Abteilung f. Hagelschlag: "New year, new happiness! This your Hedwig's sincere wish."

Prosit Neujahr

32. Photograph, Decobe 35.
    Vienna 23.5.1911. To Wohlgeborenes Fräulein Franzi Czerny,
    care of Frau Galfres-Hubermann, Wien loco, VII., Neustiftgasse
    13. I. Th. 8

35

1910.

33. Photograph. 33845/6.
   Vienna 26.7.1912. To Wohlgeborene Fräulein Mari
   Mandelburger, Pillersdorf, Post Schrattenthal bei Retz

33845/b

34. Engageo. Photograph 5019/20

Verlobt

5019/20

35. "This rose I will cherish and ever hold dear/ And a kiss for remembrance, I will give you here". Colored half-tone engraving. Th. E. L. "Theocrom" series No. 1098. Made in Germany. Charlottesville, Virginia, 21.10.1908

,,This rose I will cherish and ever hold dear"
And a kiss for remembrance, I will give you here"

36. Reproduction of a painting by Arcangelo Salvarani: *Alone at last*. Series 117/3. Crakow

39. *I'm taking piano lessons*. Half-tone engraving.
    Series: Local lovers.
    Produced by Bamforth & Co. Ltd., New York

I'M TAKING PIANO LESSONS

40. Very early "bubble" humor.
U.S.A. 24.8.1911

41, 42. Photograph. Half-tone engraving. U.S.A. About 1910.
Printers: as card 40

41, 42 Photograph. Half-tone engraving. U.S.A. About 1910.
Printers: as card 40

43. Photograph. Half-tone engraving. Printers: as cards 40-42.
From New York, N.Y., 2.2.1912.
To Englewood, New Jersey, to Miss Wilhelmine Loken,
Old Gate

44. *Le Baiser*. Photograph. Series 1106, picture 5. Printed in Germany. Koblenz, 29.10.1910, to Frl. Tilly Nordmann, Altona, Allee 254

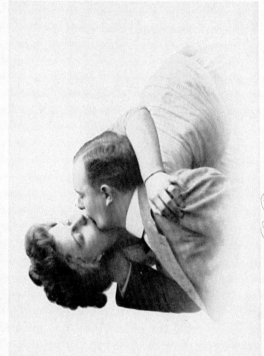

Le Baiser.

45. Half-tone engraving and color litho combined. Hamburg, 25.3.1911. To Frl. Tilly Nordmann, Altona

46, 47, 48. Photographs. Produced by P.F.B. series 2230, pictures 1-3. Printed in Germany.
Savoy Series; produced by Brown & Calder, London.
Cards unused.

How delicious is the winning.
Of a kiss at love's beginning.
When two mutual hearts are sighing
For the knot there's no untying.

2230/1

46, 47, 48. Photographs. Produced by P.F.B. series 2230, pictures
1-3. Printed in Germany.
Savoy Series; produced by Brown & Calder, London.
Cards unused.

A star of heaven you seem to me,
In shades of night who languish:
A star whose greeting glads the night,
And sweetens all my anguish.

2230/2

46, 47, 48. Photographs. Produced by P.F.B. series 2230, pictures
     1-3. Printed in Germany.
     Savoy Series; produced by Brown & Calder, London.
     Cards unused.

You lie in my arms so gladly,
On my heart so fain you rest!
You are my dearest star, love,
I am your heaven blest.

2230/3

49. *The kind of fanning I like*. U.S.A., around 1910. Photomontage. Half-tone engraving.

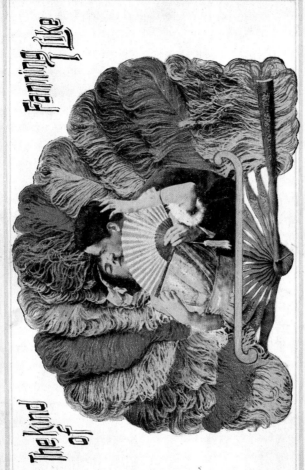

Fanning Like

The Kind of

30

50. *On the phone*. Photograph. Half-tone engraving. Produced by
    E.P.E. series 1011, picture 5. Helfenberg, 17.6.1909.
    To Hochwohlgeboren Fräulein. Hermine Herold,
    Hofratstochter, Wien VI, Wallgasse 26

51. Five small lithographs in Viennese style. Produced by B.K.W.I., series 869/10. Around 1900

52. French photomontage: *The language of colours*. Produced by DIX, series 2162

Langage des Couleurs

Tendresse rose

amour vif

rouge

espoir d'amour vert

bonheur bleu

amour constant violet

inconstant jaune

orange

on vous aime

DIX
2162

LES MARCHES
DE
L'AMOUR

54. "The Stars". Montage of photographs and drawing. France. Produced by DEDE, Paris. Series 1913

Les ASTRES

Au 7e Ciel.

Amour parfait

Lune de Miel

L'Etoile du Bonheur

Amour fugitif

DÉDÉ
PARIS
1913

55, 56. Photographs. Produced by P.C., Paris. Series 4415, pictures 1 and 3. Abbeville, 29.7.1943

55, 56. Photographs. Produced by P.C., Paris. Series 4415, pictures 1 and 3. Abbeville, 29.7.1943

57. Reproduction of a painting by Jan van Beers: *Kiss*. Half-tone engraving. Produced by M.J., Sofia, Bulgaria. 05

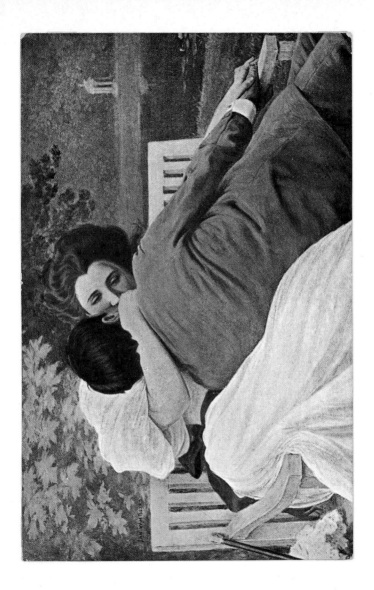

58. Reproduction of a painting by Etcheverry: *Vertige*. Half-tone engraving. Produced by M.J. Sofia. 03

59. Reproduction of a painting: *The Kiss*. Half-tone engraving.
    Printed in England: Wildt & Kray, London, N.W. No. 1717.
    Hamburg, 22.4.1911. To Fräulein Tilli Nordmann, Altona

"The Kiss"

60. Reproduction of a painting by Richard Bormeister: *The Intoxication of Love*. Half-tone engraving. Produced by Hermann Wolff, Berlin S. 59, Boppstr. 7. Series K. 1213.
Unused

61. Reproduction of a painting by R. Auer: *Passion*. Half-tone
    engraving. Art Yougoslave. Zagreb.
    Unused

R. Auer

62. *Who won?* Photograph. Half-tone engraving.
    Copyright 1909 by Taylor Art Co. Series 470

63. Reproduction of a drawing in India ink by F. von Reznicek (1868-1909): *Frontiers:* Half-tone engraving. Russian paper. Written in German: "Dearest darling—(wild) Bubi, please, once again, take care, and don't go rushing through the streets with your coat open. It's so easy to catch cold in autumn..."

64. As 63. Reznicek: *A Kiss*. "...If I were to follow my heart's desires, I'd fly straight to you..., but cold, brutal reason tells me that as you are unfortunately so busy—only you so very busy, unfortunately—I'd only be in your way. All day long you languish in "the doldrums", the evenings you'd spend in familiar friendship and love..., with me, you'd get to bed too late..."

Ф. Резничекъ, Одинъ поцѣлуй.   F von Reznicek, Ein Kuss.

65. Reproduction of an Indian ink drawing by Bill Fisher: *You—*.
    half-tone engraving. Produced by EMM. Galerie Münchner
    Meister, No. 432.
    Unused

Bill Fisher

Du —

66. Reproduction of an Indian ink drawing by Harrison Fisher:
    The Kiss. Half-tone engraving. Copyright by
    Charges Scribner's Sons.
    Produced by Reinthal and Newman, N.Y. Series 108

THE KISS

REINTHAL & NEWMAN, PUBS., N. Y.

67. Lithograph by L. v. F. Produced by Back and Schmitt,
    Vienna I, No. 1013. Correspondence card within Vienna.
    Around 1900

Wenn die Blät - - ter lei - se rau - schen

Verlag Back & Schmitt, Wien I, Nr. 1013.

68. Lithograph by Ulrich Weber. *Ueberbrettl* series Z. 2. Around 1900.
Unused

Ueber=
Brettl.

O, HASELNUSS
    O, HASELNUSS
DU BITTER BÖSER
    BAUM.

„Ueberbrettl" Ser. Z. 2

PHOTO ONLY COPYRIGHTED 1908 BY BAMFORTH & CO., NEW YORK.

I'm longing to meet you again.

70, 71, 72. Photographs. Half-tone engravings. Three cards from Bamforth and Co., Holmfirth (England) and New York. 70 and 71 from the series *Local Lovers,* 72 from the series *Bamforth's Lovers.*
Unused

IT TAKES A LOT OF THIS TO
UPSET ME

70, 71, 72. Photographs. Half-tone engravings. Three cards from
Bamforth and Co., Holmfirth (England) and New York. 70 and
71 from the series *Local Lovers*, 72 from the series *Bamforth's
Lovers*.
Unused

I'LL DO THE SAME THING OVER AGAIN

70, 71, 72. Photographs. Half-tone engravings. Three cards from
   Bamforth and Co., Holmfirth (England) and New York. 70 and
   71 from the series *Local Lovers*, 72 from the series *Bamforth's
   Lovers*.
   Unused

TAKING A LITTLE SUPPORT

73. Photograph around 1930. Produced by J.G., Paris. Series 628, picture 2.
   "To love parted, I hope it won't last much longer, and we can also be together like this. Ernst."

628/2

TON BAISER

Pour cueillir ton baiser, j'irais au bout du monde.
Un baiser fou de toi, de volupté m'inonde.

Léo
PARIS
5825

75. Photograph. Around 1930. Produced by P.C., Paris. Series
    4058, picture 2.
    Unused

UN BAISER
C'EST LE PARADIS

Mon âme connaît le délire,
Et mon pauvre cerveau chavire,
Par ton amour tout étourdi...
Ton baiser, c'est le Paradis !

P.C.
PARIS
4058/2

76. Hand-colored photograph. About 1930. Produced by P.C.,
    Paris. Series 2616.
    Unused

77. Color lithograph: *150 an hour!*

150 à l'heure!!

195.

78. Color litho, relief print. *Love's golden dream!*
    England, around 1905. Series No. 6310 Relief

Love's golden dream!

He's rather too young!

79. Color litho, relief print. England, about 1905.
    Mrs. J. Johns, 14 High Street, Eveshaw, Worcestershire. "Hope this postcard don't offend you."

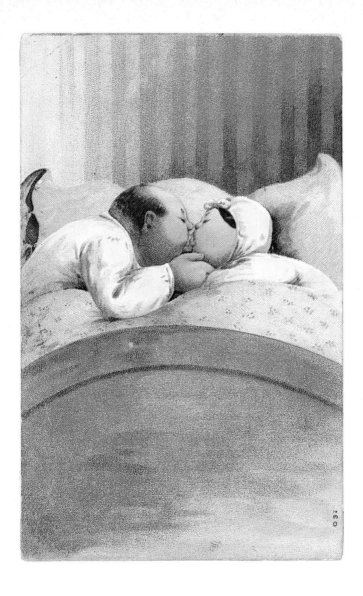

80. Photograph. Fotobrom, Vienna VII, NPG (Neue
    Photographische Gesellschaft), No. 324.
    Mönichkirchen, 29.4.1913. Wohlgeboren Fräulein Mizzi Karl-
    inger, Wien IX/2, Nussdorfer Strasse 16. "Pity I don't know"
    Frau Ridi's address, otherwise I'd have sent this card to her. Saucy!
    she'd have squealed again. We're going to Krumbach today.
    A teacher's being buried there..."

324